Original title:
Bangles and Beyond

Copyright © 2025 Creative Arts Management OÜ
All rights reserved.

Author: Nathaniel Blackwood
ISBN HARDBACK: 978-1-80586-102-7
ISBN PAPERBACK: 978-1-80586-574-2

Trinkets of Tradition

In a corner shop they shine,
A pile of colors, all so fine.
Jangling as you sway your hips,
Question: Do they add to your quips?

Each one tells a tale, it's true,
Of dances past and tea for two.
Whispers of history gleam so bright,
When you wear them, it feels just right.

Curves of Color and Light

Curvy shapes that sparkle and dance,
Catch the eye, they start a romance.
With every twist, they tell a joke,
At parties, they always provoke.

Swirling tones of pink and green,
Making every outfit feel like a dream.
You can't help but laugh and sway,
Each piece has its own silly say.

The Story of a Thousand Bangles

A thousand stories wrapped in gold,
Of mischief, laughter, and tales retold.
You wear them like a badge of cheer,
Echoes of joy that bring us near.

Crackling sound, a funny beat,
Dancing to rhythm under your feet.
Every clash is a comedic rhyme,
Time-traveling back through space and time.

Kaleidoscope of Wearable Wonders

A kaleidoscope so bright and bold,
With every jingle, a story told.
Round and round, they twirl and glide,
They're the quirky friends you don't hide.

Tickled pink and tickled blue,
When you wear them, they outshine you.
Giggles echo in every thread,
Adventures linger, never dead.

The Art of Adornment

In a crowd, she twirls and spins,
Clinking sounds, where fun begins.
Her wrists jingle like a seasoned band,
Making music, oh so unplanned.

Friends ask, 'What's that sound so loud?'
She smiles, 'Just me, feeling proud!'
With every clash, her spirit sings,
A symphony of shiny things.

Splintered Reflections

Look at her, with sparkling flair,
Reflecting light, like a disco ball in the air.
'What's your secret?' her friends implore,
'Just wear more clinks, you'll never bore!'

Each piece tells stories, some old, some new,
Like an awkward dance, in a dazzling view.
She slips, she trips, but laughs it away,
Her charm shines brighter, come what may.

Echoed Moments in Metal

Every step echoes, a rhythmic beat,
A merry festival for the feet.
With each little jingle, she spreads her cheer,
Like a one-woman band, you'll want her near.

Footloose and fancy, her spirit is light,
But watch out for those who envy her height!
When they ask for tips on how to shine,
She says, 'Just wave your arms, and you'll be fine!'

Luminous Threads of Life

In the park, she struts with pride,
Shiny strands, her joy can't hide.
Every twist and turn, a giggly show,
Wherever she goes, the laughter will flow.

Her friends join in, a colorful crew,
Dressed like rainbows—oh what a view!
With every jangle, the day feels bright,
They're off to conquer the world, in pure delight.

Silent Statements of Beauty

In a whisper of glimmering hue,
They dance on wrists, so bright and true.
A clink and a jingle, a story unfolds,
Of nights full of laughter and tales never told.

With each playful flick, they jive and sway,
Adventures of life in their shiny display.
Who needs a crown when your arms shine bright?
Royalty's charm wrapped in pure delight.

Wrapped in Radiance

Oh, the sparkle that graces each hand,
Like tiny confetti from a joyful land.
They clatter and sparkle, a sound so absurd,
A symphony crafted from laughter unheard.

As I walk down the street, they twirl in cheer,
Like tiny little dancers, they bring in the year.
Wristwear for wittiness, they surely convey,
Hold on to your hats, they lead us astray.

The Heritage Within

In layers of culture, they giggle and gleam,
Each one a relic from a forgotten dream.
Traditions wrapped up in colorful bands,
Sometimes they giggle at clumsy hands.

Grandma's tales live in their jingle and clink,
While I try to balance and not spill my drink.
Heritage shines, yet it moves with the flow,
A quirky appraiser of how much I know.

Eternal Charms of Delight

They sparkle 'round arms, a whimsical touch,
A joke on my wrist, I never get too much.
They josh and they jive, they never stop playing,
When life's a bit dull, they start the relaying.

Catch-me-if-you-can, they tease and they twirl,
In a dance of allure, they give life a whirl.
A cheer for the moments that make us all bright,
These charming companions bring laughter in sight.

Roaming the World of Adornments

In a shop filled with glitter, I peep,
A rainbow of treasures, oh so steep.
I try on a bangle, it squeezes tight,
My wrist looks like a turkey, what a sight!

The lady behind the counter says, "Wow!"
Laughing so hard, I nearly take a bow.
She hands me a necklace shaped like a fish,
Now I look like a walking stylish dish.

A charm in one hand, earrings in the other,
A fashion clash like no sister or brother.
I twirl and I spin, to the music I sway,
With a hat, a scarf—I'm turning heads today!

In this world of adornment, I've lost all shame,
My style's a funny and whimsical claim.
Each trinket a tale, each piece a surprise,
A jester of fashion, I wear with pride!

Celebrating Craft and Culture

In a market bustling, colors collide,
Crafty creations parade with pride.
Each trinket sings of a tale well spun,
Laughter and culture, merging as one.

A pair of earrings, sparkly and bright,
They dance on my ears, such a silly sight.
A local artisan winks, 'What do you think?'
I say, "They look good, but they might just blink!"

Around me, the laughter, a fabric of cheer,
With every smile shared, my worries disappear.
Where crafts meet jest, and culture entwines,
I strut like a peacock, drinking good wines.

With each purchase made, my wallet takes flight,
But who needs cash when you're feeling so right?
In the world of crafts, I'm a quirky delight,
Celebrating life, with charm and with bite!

An Odyssey in Bracelets

I'm on a quest for the perfect wrist wear,
Plastic and gold, and some without care.
Each bangle a story, each clasp holds a laugh,
A friend calls me 'Jenga'—best not to graph!

One slips and it jingles, a mess in a flash,
I trip on my bling, it makes quite the crash.
A lady stops, chuckling, "You're quite a sight!"
I grin and reply, "Only on this bright night!"

From pearls to leather, my arm starts to weigh,
Each trip is an adventure, come join on the play.
My bracelets are chatting, gossiping loud,
"Look at that dork, she's so very proud!"

In an odyssey, truly, fashion leads the way,
With every turn, new treasures on display.
A chorus of color, my arm tells a tale,
Of laughter and whimsy, in style, I set sail!

The Kiss of Color and Glass

In a world made of shimmer, I take my first step,
Rings here, and there, not one I can prep.
Beads of bright color, they beckon with glee,
I stumble, I bumble, this fashion's not free!

A glass bracelet sparkles like stars in the night,
But when I put it on, it slips out of sight.
My clumsiness grows, and the shopkeeper grins,
As I trip on my own charm, chaos begins!

A medley of shades, they twirl and they whirl,
I'm caught in a whirlwind, let's give it a whirl.
The laughter resounds as I catch a cool breeze,
With elegance lost, but hey, I'm still at ease!

With a wink to the mirrors, I dance to the beat,
In colors and laughter, my heart skips a beat.
So here's to the fun, the laughter, the cheer,
With every new trinket, let's raise a cold beer!

The Art of Adorning the Everyday

A shimmer on my wrist, I say,
Is better than a dull old tray.
Each twist and jingle brings such cheer,
A dance of colors, oh so clear.

My cat's confused, it thinks it's prey,
It pounces on my arm for play.
With every jangle, it does flee,
Who knew that cats dislike bling spree?

In mornings bright, I match the hues,
With mismatched styles, I can't refuse.
Some think I'm mad, but that's okay,
In clashing glory, I'll sway my way.

Embrace of the Tangled Thread

When threads entwine, it feels like fate,
I laugh at knots that dare sedate.
A loop here, a tangle there,
A friendship forged in fabric's flair.

With every twist, I tell a tale,
Of lost socks and a wayward snail.
Who knew a bead could spark such fun?
An artful mess, my chores outrun.

In a crafty storm, I'm quite the queen,
Though scissors lurk, my laugh's routine.
For each mishap, a giggle's born,
And in this chaos, my heart's adorned.

Jewel Adornments

My jewels jingle, quite the ruckus,
They mock my silence, what a circus!
Dancing on my neck with glee,
As I trip over my own two feet.

A pendant swings; it's got some nerve,
To lead me into a crazy curve.
I laugh and twirl, a clumsy queen,
With dazzling views, I'm never mean.

Those gems and charms, so bold and bright,
Draw laughter from the left and right.
In every shimmer, a tale unfolds,
Of joy in chaos, and sparkly golds.

Whispers of Sparkling Circles

Round and round, they seem to say,
'Hey, don't forget to laugh today!'
A circle here, a circle there,
Join the party, without a care.

With every clink, a chuckle's heard,
They gossip softly, just a word.
An earring slips; oh what a sight!
I'm a walking joke, delightfully slight.

In circles bright, my mood's the theme,
Sparkling tales like frothy cream.
With each adornment, I claim my crown,
In this funny world, I'll never frown.

A Tapestry of Tradition

In a box of childhood dreams,
Sparkles wait with crooked seams.
Mom says wear them, look so sweet,
But my wrist just can't compete!

A clash of colors, oh what fun,
Clinking sounds like a playful pun.
Neighbors peek, they grin and stare,
As I wobble, unaware of care!

Jewelry's Generational Echo

Grandma's treasures, shiny and bright,
Tales of battles, laughter, and fright.
I wear her gems with such great pride,
But they slide off; oh, what a ride!

Mom beams as I put them on,
Saying, "Those are mine!" - I feel like a con.
Her styles clash, but mine's pure fun,
A family feud where no one's won!

Worn Through the Ages

With every layer, I feel the weight,
Of history twinkling, isn't it fate?
My friends arrive with arms of style,
I just laugh; it's been a while!

We dance like fools, beads in a whirl,
Catching light, like a sparkly pearl.
Old tales tumble, mixed with laughter,
As we pose for the future, 'til after!

The Ballet of Adornment

A pirouette in rhinestones so bright,
Dancing like a disco ball in flight.
With every twirl, they jingle with glee,
An ensemble cast, just my friends and me!

Tapping toes and flailing arms,
Accidental charm, here's where it warms.
Except for a snap! Oh what's that sound?
Jewelry's pout when it hits the ground!

Whispers of Worn Adornments

In a drawer of dust and dreams,
Lies a treasure, or so it seems.
Forgotten gems of past delight,
Whisper tales of wild party night.

Each glint a giggle, each clank a cheer,
Once so shiny, now strange to hear.
They jingle loud in a silenced home,
Like they're plotting how to roam.

"My dear, where have you been?" they sigh,
"Let's recreate the dance, oh my!"
A pair of loops with stories old,
Shining still, yet slightly cold.

So grab the jar, unleash the fun,
Let clashing colors dance and run.
Adornments worn, let laughter reign,
Their echoes sweet, like a candy cane.

Echoes from the Arm

Oh the arm, a stage for flair,
With echoes red, blue, and some silverware.
I shake it once, it rattles loud,
Fashion's jester, drawing a crowd.

A bump, a twist, a squishy sound,
Dancing circles, joy unbound.
Every bang a story told,
Of ice cream fights and bravado bold.

"Would you look at that!" the neighbors gasp,
As colors clash in a joyful clasp.
A joyful noise, a rebel's cheer,
I wave my arm—come join us here!

So put on your rings, don't hesitate,
Join this party; it's never too late.
Let's rattle and roll, wear our charms,
And create more echoes from our arms.

The Dance of Colored Circles

In the night, a vibrant show,
Circles twirl, each one a glow.
They spin and twinkle, side by side,
In this dance, we take great pride.

Red and green form the perfect pair,
While blue and yellow swirl in air.
Bouncing lightly, oh what a sight,
They form a circus, pure delight.

"Oh, look at me!" a purple spins,
"Watch out for joy, it always wins!"
With every twist, a giggle flows,
A dance of colors, see how it glows!

So gather 'round this playful spree,
With circles hopping, wild and free.
Let laughter lead, let worries flee,
Join the dance of who we can be!

Clinking Memories Unveiled

In a box tucked safe from view,
Clinking memories come anew.
They jingle with a childhood tune,
As I find them under the moon.

A shimmer here, a twinkle there,
Reminders of laughter, beyond compare.
"Remember me?" they start to sing,
As I recall that joyful fling.

Each little sound a story brings,
Of all the silly, fun-filled things.
They rattled during games of tag,
In every color, not one drab rag.

So let them out, let the music play,
Roll back the years, let's dance today.
With clinks and laughs that never fade,
These memories are not ones to trade.

Legacy in Luminous Layers

Stacked high like a tower, oh what a sight,
Each charm whispers secrets, shining so bright.
Worn by the grandmas, kids in delight,
Even the cat thinks it's her night!

Gold and silver, a jingle parade,
Every clink resounds with stories conveyed.
Should I see a ghost or simply be swayed?
Oh, these shiny wonders never fade!

Inscriptions of Time on Skin

Marks of adventures, tales etched with glee,
Oops, that one's from last year's wild spree!
Lawn mower scars, and a stubbed toe spree,
Count all my treasures—what a sight to see!

Each notch a reminder, bold deeds and fun,
I laughed, I cried, oh where to run?
With every tick-tock, the stories are spun,
Who needs a tattoo? I'm more than one!

Reflections of Radiant History

Look in the mirror, what a funny frame,
A glittery circus of each workday game.
Dancing reflections, each shines like fame,
Standing in awe, how'd I get this lame?

Glimmers and glances, a festival here,
Who wore it best? Oh dear, never fear!
Cousin's bright light, oh she's so sincere,
While my clutter sparkles, I volunteer!

The Languages of Lovely Adornments

Chirps of colors, a vibrant brigade,
Peals of laughter, in the shimmer we wade.
Silent conversations, the looks we trade,
When jewels do the talking, no need to evade!

Each piece has a sparkle, a wink and a grin,
Sassy statements say, let the fun begin!
In this jewelry jungle, I'm lost in the din,
With every shiny treasure, I dive right in!

Embracing Tradition in Elegance

In ancestral boxes, treasures hide,
Each twist and turn, a joyful ride.
Dancing wrist, it clinks and clanks,
With every move, the laughter pranks.

Grandma's look is a wondrous sight,
With colors bold, it feels so light.
Hiding secrets within each curve,
A fashion statement, we observe.

Under the sun, they catch the dance,
A glimmer here, a sparkly chance.
Rumbling pockets, oh what a sound,
Who knew joy could so freely abound?

So let us wear them, don't delay,
With every jingle, we're here to play.
In playful harmony, here we glide,
With elegance and smiles, side by side.

Chimes of Heritage and Heart

Ringing bright with joy around,
Each jingle sings, a playful sound.
Little hearts join in the spree,
As tales untold float blissfully.

Tiny hands reach out in glee,
To hold the past so carefully.
Mismatched pieces tell us clear,
Life is silly, hold it dear.

With every clash against the skin,
An adventure waits where we begin.
Folks may stop and raise an eye,
But who's to judge our joyful sky?

Thus we dance, a vibrant dream,
With laughter loud, we reign supreme.
In every flicker, bright and bold,
A legacy of joy untold.

Shadows of Shimmering Dreams

Beneath the lights, the magic fades,
While friends swap stories in charades.
A shadow here, a sparkle there,
Who needs a throne when you have flair?

Childlike giggles in the night,
With every shine, a sheer delight.
A flick, a twist, the shadows play,
While we giggle and sway away.

Wristbands rattle with every jest,
Crafty tales from the very best.
"Did you see that?" whispers the crowd,
As laughter erupts, silly yet loud.

In this circle, we're all a gold,
Earning happiness, keeping bold.
So dance and twirl, let shadows gleam,
In the heart of night, chase the dream.

When Jewels Tell Tales

A little twinkle from her ear,
She spins a yarn, we lean in near.
"Once I had a charming quest,"
With every story, we're truly blessed.

The jewels wink and blink a tune,
As if they're giggling at the moon.
"Once I danced on a tiger's tail,"
Her laughter rings, a blissful trail.

We gather 'round for every cheer,
Because laughter's spark is always near.
Stories unfold like magic dust,
It's fun to share, we simply must!

So lift your glass, let's toast tonight,
To every tale that brings delight.
With sparkling gems, we laugh and sway,
In joyous hearts, we dance and play.

Threading Joy Through Time

In a shop where colors twine,
A twist of fate makes fingers shine.
The clerk says, 'Try this sparkly hue!'
But really, it's a sneaky shoe.

They jangle and clink, a sound so bright,
But step on toes, oh what a fright!
Each set tells tales of laughter loud,
While I trip over this glittering crowd.

Rolls of ribbon and pearls abound,
Yet I'm tangled up without a sound.
I tried to dance, but who would guess,
My outfit's now a tangled mess!

With every step, a jolly sway,
Lost in charms, I laugh and play.
An accessory meant for delight,
Turns me into quite the sight!

Ephemeral Elegance

A shimmer here, a twinkle there,
I put them on with little care.
They slip and slide, what fun to chase,
A runaway gem, oh, what a race!

Wearing elegance with charm so bold,
But off they fly like birds of gold.
I capture one, then lose the next,
My fashion sense? A comedy text!

Sparkling beads on my silly knee,
A fashion faux pas, who'd agree?
I strut my stuff, though arms are bare,
And trip on beads, oh how I dare!

Elegant chaos, a sight unseen,
With every twist, I'm just a queen.
So here I twirl, absurd yet proud,
In this joyous chaos, I stand loud!

Ancestral Adornments

Grandma's gems, an ancient charm,
They wobble and jostle, causing alarm.
She chuckles and says, 'Wear them with glee!'
But really, I'm limping, oh woe is me!

A string of history, tales galore,
Yet one slipped off to explore the floor.
I dive to rescue, arms in a twist,
And knock over a vase I just can't miss!

Each piece whispers stories from the past,
While I spill my drink in a jolly blast.
A fashionista? Nah, I'm just a klutz,
Mixing elegance with some big ol' buts!

Though they sparkle, there's no debate,
I wear them like trophies of my fate.
With every fumble, I grin wide,
Ancestral flair with zany pride!

Circular Whimsy

Round and round, they spin with glee,
A whirl of laughter surrounding me.
I try to dance, and oh what fun,
I'm gone before I'm really done!

The siren call of silvery rings,
Each little jingle, a song that sings.
But as I twist, a clatter resounds,
A wedding cupcake on the ground!

In my quest for circular flair,
I crash through clouds of whipped cream air.
Friends all giggle, they can't get enough,
Maybe it's time to rethink my stuff!

So here I glide in my shiny gear,
Each turn a spectacle, loud and clear.
With laughter trailing as I embrace,
This absurd twist, oh what a grace!

Adorned Stories of the Past

In a box of trinkets, tales unwind,
Each jingling sound, a giggle behind.
My grandmother's pearls, a frightful sight,
She wore them to dance, embracing the night.

The bracelets jingle, a merry tune,
As I try them on, I break a balloon.
With every twist, a laugh echoes loud,
Fashion faux pas, yet I stand proud.

A necklace from auntie, slightly askew,
I swear it's a snake, not jewelry new.
It whispers secrets, all tangled in glee,
Adorned memories, that tickle me.

So here's to the past, in gold and in thread,
Each piece has a story, a life that's been led.
With laughter and folly, I wear them today,
In the grand old parade, we frolic and play.

Beads of Time and Rhythm

Beads strung together, a wobbly line,
Like my morning dance, oh so divine.
Each one tells a tale, a chuckle or two,
Fell off my wrist, but it wished it knew.

A clatter, a rattle, they leap and they bounce,
Join the conga, I seem to renounce.
Laughing with beads, that stick to my hair,
A rhythm of chaos, but I do not care.

Colors so vibrant, they tussle and fight,
In a dance-off of shine, they're out of my sight.
The disco ball chuckles, "What are you wearing?"
A mismatched affair, but oh, so declaring!

Time whirls in circles, each bead a delight,
With giggles and sparkles, we sway through the night.
These beads of mischief, they twinkle with cheer,
Wobbling through life, let's raise a loud cheer!

Circles of Light in Motion

A dazzling arm, all shimmery spins,
With circles of laughter, let the fun begin.
Each twirl of my wrist, the sparkles entwine,
A dance of the silly, both merry and fine.

The sun hits just right, oh what a sight,
Like tiny UFOs taking flight.
With each twinkle and jiggle, I'm feeling alive,
Mischief in jewelry, oh how we thrive!

I whirl past the cats, their tails all askew,
They think I'm a comet coming right through.
I trip on my dress, land flat on the ground,
But the circles keep spinning, a joy to be found.

So here's to the gems, that dance through the day,
In laughter and chaos, they frolic and play.
With diamonds and giggles, our spirits ignite,
In circles of joy, we twirl through the night.

The Jewelry of Journeys

A suitcase of beads, we set off to roam,
Each necklace a story from far away home.
With anklets that jingle, we travel with flair,
Making memories shiny, more than a wear.

In markets of laughter, I barter and trade,
For a glittering brooch that won't quite cascade.
It's stuck on my shirt, a fashionable fright,
Who knew a butterfly could add to my plight?

From beaches to mountains, the tales don't end,
With each borrowed piece, my style I blend.
A charm from a stranger, a wink and a smile,
This journey of jewels makes life worthwhile.

So let's collect laughter, in patterns and lines,
For every adventure, a sparkle that shines.
In travels of humor, we find what we seek,
The jewels of our journey are unique and chic!

In the Shadow of Inner Beauty

Round and shiny, they catch the light,
Jangling laughter, such a sight!
A dance on wrists, a playful tease,
Making even grumpy folks feel at ease.

Each one whispers a tale or two,
Of awkward flings and spills of stew.
Who knew bling could make us trip?
It's hard to walk with a shaky grip!

They shine like stars in everyday wear,
Sometimes just noise in the family's air.
Oh the joy and sound they bring,
Life's quirkiest, clink-clinking bling!

When I'm grumpy, they hit the floor,
Rolling and tumbling; such a score!
A jolly mess and a giggle fit,
In their playful chaos, I admit!

The Embrace of Color

A splash of hue, I wear them bright,
Like disco balls in the morning light.
They jingle-jangle with every sway,
Making gray skies fade away.

Each shade tells a story untold,
Of mishaps, laughter, and friends of old.
Pink for blushes, green for glee,
Yellow for chaos, oh let it be!

Sometimes they clash in a colorful mess,
A sight that's anything but finesse.
A rainbow riot on my arm,
Who knew bright colors could cause such charm?

They twinkle at night, with a wink and cheer,
Chasing away all my daily fear.
They're like party guests wrapped around,
Bringing humor, so joy is found!

Circular Pathways of Emotion

Movements swirl in a jolly dance,
Circles of laughter, quite the chance!
Round and round, they take a spin,
Bouncing thoughts and giggles within.

A clattering echo with each grand step,
A tripping tune, what's next, misstep?
Joyful chaos on my limbs lays,
Like a circus, full of play!

These hoops of joy, like life's great wheel,
Every twist and turn, another squeal.
With laughter echoing all around,
Such a twirly, whirly, merry sound!

Each shake whispers secrets divine,
Of clumsy dances and spilled wine.
In circles we twirl through smiles galore,
Life's silly journey we can't ignore!

Glistening Journeys

Across the market, I strut with flair,
Jingling trails of joy in the air.
Each step takes me to places unknown,
With friendships formed, laughter grown.

A sparkle here, a shimmer there,
They brighten paths with vibrant care.
Oh, the stories they could tell,
Of adventures that went exceptionally well!

I wave to strangers; we bond through sound,
In this journey, joy knows no bounds.
With glittering tales of mishaps and fun,
Every sparkly moment under the sun.

So here's to the journeys, big and small,
With each clink echoing, I stand tall.
Together we twinkle, we giggle and play,
Life's merry adventure, come what may!

Delicate Echoes of Existence

In a drawer they dance, with clinks and clatters,
Whispers of good times, and unexpected matters.
Like tiny moons orbiting my wrist,
What's the point of wearing them if they can't twist?

From brunch to the disco, they jingle and jive,
One little twist, and oh! They come alive.
But during a coffee, they clink and spill,
My latte's now accessorized, it's quite the thrill!

A tangled mess after a wild night out,
Finding the culprit? Oh, without a doubt!
Each piece a story, from dance floor to couch,
Keeping secrets like a persistent slouch.

They laugh in the sunlight, there's mischief in every hue,
Like friends at a party, cheers to the crew!
Wrapped in joy, they shimmer and play,
Oh delightful echoes, brighten my day!

Luminescent Stories of Spirit

In the moonlight they shimmer, a glittering tale,
Of trips to the market and avoiding a fail.
Caught in the door? Oh, what a surprise!
A blast of laughter, they've covered my eyes!

With each gentle jingle, a story unfold,
Of secrets they carry, both new and old.
A fashion statement, or a snack attack?
Sometimes they help, and sometimes they lack!

They sparkle with stories, of dance moves gone wrong,
Of attempting to salsa, with a twisty little song.
And when I forget them? My wrist feels so bare,
Like a fish out of water, gasping for air!

In colors so bright, they gleam and they shine,
Each piece a character, perfectly divine.
With laughter surrounding, let's give them a cheer,
For every mishap, they're always near!

A Dance of Grace and Glisten

Oh glittering friends, let's hit the floor,
In synchronized chaos, let's shake it some more!
With mismatched colors, we whirl and we twirl,
A fashion faux pas? No need for a curl!

I slip on my shoes, and then all goes wild,
Each jingle is giggles, I'm the happy child.
Who knew that my arm would steal the whole show?
As I flail with my hands, my style would bestow!

A bracelet gets caught on a friendly old shirt,
I tug and I yank, but oh! What a hurt!
Laughter erupts, so let's dance with glee,
In the symphony of sparkle, oh won't you join me?

As stars in the sky join in the fun,
These pieces of joy will never be done.
With grace and with glisten, we'll twinkle tonight,
A joyful explosion, what a silly sight!

Timeless Melodies of Adornment

Each lovely piece holds a melody sweet,
With a hop and a skip, they tap to my beat.
Worn on my wrist like a catchy little tune,
They shine with a hope, like the sun and the moon!

At work they distract, oh, a curious sound,
While I'm typing away, they rattle around!
"Is that a bell?" my boss raised an eye,
I grin and I giggle, "Yeah, it's just my style!"

Stuck in my coat when I try to unwind,
As I tumble and fumble, they leave me behind.
Each piece a reminder of moments so grand,
In the rhythm of laughter, together we stand!

So here's to the jingles, the flair and the frolic,
With every new movement, the joy is symbolic.
Life's too short to wear dull and plain,
Let's dance with our hearts, and let laughter reign!

Chapter of Charm

In a store filled with colors, so bright,
I tripped on a box, what a sight!
Jewels rolled away, laughing like kids,
"Chase us!" they shouted, oh dear heavens hid!

Neighbors all stared, what a grand show,
With gems on my face, like a disco glow.
Each piece of my outfit, a puzzle, you see,
Who knew that style could be so wild and free?

Twirled like a dancer, I showed off my flair,
With clips in my hair, and a sparkly bear.
The cat joined the party, oh what a strife,
He wore all my treasures, claiming his life!

Yet as I stumbled, my charm took a hit,
Each bauble just laughed—how clever, how witty!
They glittered with glee, oh what a delight,
A spectacle formed in the afternoon light!

The Language of Adornments

In the land of trinkets, words seem to dance,
Each piece a secret, each clasp a chance.
A necklace whispered, 'Let's go for ice cream!'
While bangles frolicked, and sang like a dream.

My earrings conspired, with a giggle and cheer,
"Let's sparkle this party! Loud and clear!"
They jangled together, oh what a ruckus,
Some danced on the table, saying, "Look at us!"

"Let's start a revolution!" cried out my charm,
"A bling-bling brigade, let's cause some alarm!"
So we marched through the streets, shining like stars,
Gathering smiles, giggles, we traveled far.

Then came a cat, adorned with a crown,
He meowed like a king, with jewels renowned.
A laugh in his eyes, he joined our parade,
In the tale of adornments, epic adventures made!

Decorative Legacies

Once there was a bracelet, a tale to share,
It claimed to be ancient, with stories to spare.
"It danced with pharaohs!" it chattered with glee,
But I'm quite certain, it just lived with me.

Each gem had a story, each bead had a laugh,
One said, "I was lost in a bubble bath!"
So together they giggled, recounting their past,
Creating a legacy, a spell that would last.

My necklace proclaimed, "I've seen it all!"
"From garden parties to the grandest ball!"
While the earrings just chirped, "We're timeless for sure!"

"Fashion's our playground, life's a great tour!"

As laughter erupted, my treasures did twirl,
In a decorative dance, oh what a whirl!
With every embellishment, a life I could weave,
In this legacy of laughter, I'd surely believe!

Curated Forever

In a box full of laughter, a collection so sweet,
A treasure of whimsy, a rhythmic heartbeat.
With glimmers and sparkles, they told me their dreams,
Adventures entwined in their metallic schemes.

An old ring remembered, it chuckled with pride,
"I sat in a drawer, with nowhere to hide!"
But now it's a star, shining bright in the light,
Scrambling for attention, a most curious sight.

"Let's curate the evening!" my brooch gave a cheer,
"Let's hang out in style; make sparkles appear!"
So the pins voted yes, in a very loud way,
Their plans for the night? A dazzling display!

The cat, quite amused, joined in the parade,
Draped in my treasures, a hefty charade.
With jewels a-jingle, we danced through the night,
A curated fiesta, pure fun and delight!

Reflections of Cultural Splendor

In a market of color, I twirl and sway,
My arms jingle softly, come join the play.
Grandma rolls her eyes, says, 'Not again!',
But I can't resist that shimmering train!

Neighbors spark gossip, old stories unfold,
'Why wear just one? You must wear a fold!'
I stack them up high, let the laughter ignite,
For nothing's more bright than a colorful sight.

Uncle thinks they're weapons, but he's misunderstood,
While I dream of kingdoms, of bangles and wood.
The girls all agree: more is simply more!
And hidden beneath is a fashion galore!

Oh, the world is a stage, and my arms take the lead,
Where every twinkle speaks a language indeed.
Each jingle a secret, a story of cheer,
In this circus of colors, there's nothing to fear!

A Dance with Time

Tick-tock goes the clock, as my arm starts to bling,
I dance with the shadows, ready to swing.
'What time do you call this?' my father inquires,
But I'm busy dazzling like fireworks' fires!

Each clink got its rhythm, it leads me astray,
In a whirl of confusion, I'm lost in the sway.
'Is that your wrist or a band's rock concert?'
Don't interrupt the magic, it's pure, I assert!

Time runs in circles, I let it all flow,
With each little jingle, my spirit will glow.
So I shimmy and shake, twirling stories anew,
Life's just a dance, let the laughter ensue!

Maybe I'll trip, sing and laugh all the same,
But the echoes of joy are what fuel the flame.
For in this wild dance, from dusk until dawn,
I wear my bright treasures while playing along!

Encircled in Elegance

With every soft jingle, I step on the scene,
Draped in vibrancy, a shimmering queen.
My mother's permission? Ha! I've done it again,
Wearing her treasures, I'm more than a ten!

'Is it bold or a blunder?' my neighbor will guess,
Yet my outfit clearly screams, 'Why settle for less?'
Each layer I wear is a story of fun,
Like a rainbow in sun, at sweet day's long run.

I run by the fountain, they all start to stare,
'Is that a fierce fashion or is she just rare?'
Though elegance whispers, I giggle with glee,
Witty and bright—what a sight to see!

Round and round I go, a whirlwind of flair,
Sprinkling some laughter, how little they care.
Heartbeats and jewels, who needs to pretend?
In this circle of style, let the laughter blend!

A Mosaic of Meaning

In a world full of colors, I create with delight,
Each piece tells a tale, as I dance into night.
A patchwork of laughter, where joy interweaves,
My bracelet's a canvas, spun from dreams and leaves.

A glance at the stories wrapped tight on my wrist,
'What's the meaning in that?' they can't resist.
I shrug with a smile, say, 'Why must I choose?
Every color's a memory; I'll never lose!'

Neighbors drop hints, 'Are you jesting with style?'
Each wink says it's crazy, but oh, wait a while!
When I shake and I twirl like a dervish so grand,
These pieces remind me of faraway lands.

So bring on the sparkle, the giggles, the flair,
For life is a mosaic of dreams we all share.
With each twist and jingle, I find my own tune,
In this joyous adventure, we'll dance to the moon!

Chronicles of Ornate Whispers

In a cupboard, treasures hide,
All the colors, oh, they bide,
When they jingle, it's a cheer,
Making everyone come near.

With a twist and a little shake,
Jokes arise, we can't forsake,
Every clink tells a witty tale,
Of grandmas' antics, never stale.

At parties, watch them dance and gleam,
Like fireflies in a wild dream,
Tickling toes and making noise,
Our laughter equals all the joys.

So here's to all the quirks we wear,
Each piece has a story, that's so rare,
In shiny worlds where we all connect,
Ornate whispers we can't neglect.

Kaleidoscope Dreams

In a whirlwind of vibrant hues,
Hiding laughter, sharing news,
Swirling colors, oh what a sight,
Each a giggle, pure delight.

A twist of gold and glint of green,
Making mundane moments seem keen,
Life's a dance, and they lead us,
With a sparkle, they tease and fuss.

Round and round, they clink and chime,
Creating chaos, but that's just fine,
Each tiny piece, a joke in hand,
Bringing smiles in a quirky band.

In this magical, vivid spree,
We find laughter, wild and free,
With every glance, a joke is found,
In kaleidoscope dreams, joy abounds.

Timeless Treasures

In a box, the memories glow,
Stitching tales we love to show,
Each trinket hides a giggle or two,
Timeless treasures, always new.

Feathers, gems, and sparkles bright,
Every piece is pure delight,
From jingling laughter in the breeze,
To silly dances that all please.

Once in a while, they play a game,
Turning shy, but never lame,
With a twirl, they lead the fun,
Where every moment is a pun.

So cherish these, the quirks we love,
Shiny snippets, like stars above,
In every gleam, a story spins,
Timeless treasures where joy begins.

The Artful Touch

With every clink, a story's told,
In a swirling dance, they bold,
The artful touch, in gleeful ways,
Bringing laughter on our days.

Playful twists and shades to flaunt,
Making moments, oh so vaunt,
They whisper secrets, tease and jest,
Wearing humor as their best.

In the shuffle and playful cheer,
We find joy, and everyone draws near,
Catch the sparkle, let it flow,
An artful touch, it steals the show.

So come together, join the game,
Each jingle, we can't quite tame,
In this festive, joyful dance,
The artful touch gives life a chance.

Threads of Culture Woven

In a market full of colors bright,
She tried on every piece in sight.
With laughter ringing through the air,
Her cousin's outfit was quite a scare!

The old man nodded, like a sage,
Said, "Style has no limit at any age!"
Yet as he twisted, those beads went flying,
An army of pearls joined in the prying.

With every twist and jingle's chime,
They all declared, "This should be crime!"
But who could resist that playful bling?
They danced as if they were the spring.

So here's to trinkets and all their cheer,
A sparkle here, a shimmer near.
In trends so wild, like a jester's spree,
Life's a circus, let it be free!

Rhythm of the Raindrop's Fall

Pitter-patter on the tin roof loud,
Dancers gather, forming a crowd.
With umbrellas flipped and colors bright,
They twirl and spin, a comical sight.

A lady slipped, what a flurry!
Rain-soaked socks, oh what a worry!
A gentle splash, laughter erupts,
Dance like raindrops, just let it disrupt!

Oh, how they step, some slip, some glide,
In puddles deep, joy will abide.
With laughter ringing, they kick and play,
This soggy day won't get in their way.

So join the shindig beneath the storm,
Let your heart be merry, let your spirits warm.
For in every drop, with silly delight,
Is a chance at joy, hold on tight!

The Circle of Life's Embrace

In a gathering where chaos reigns,
A group dons styles that warps all chains.
With outfits swirling, colors collide,
Fashion faux pas? They wear with pride!

Granny tries her granddaughter's shoes,
Trips and stumbles—ample views!
Yet in the fall, she finds her flair,
"Back to the dance floor, I'm still a bear!"

The fashion police, they gasp in shock,
As uncles flaunt their mismatched flock.
Yet every twirl, the joy expands,
Life's too short for boring brands!

With each embrace, mistaken or true,
They leap like flamingos, a colorful crew.
In this circle, vibrant and wild,
A reminder to dance, not just be styled!

Harmony in Iridescent Swirls

In a world of shimmer, they prance and sway,
With blinding colors, come join the fray.
A mix of patterns, styles of delight,
They twang like strings in the warm moonlight.

A hat one way, shoes mismatched tight,
Yet no one's hiding—oh, what a sight!
Children giggle, elders cheer,
Showcasing treasures, oh so dear.

Even the cat dons a shiny cape,
Looks like royalty, a comical shape!
Whiskers twitching, strutting around,
In the realm of style, it's joy they found.

So let the colors create a mess,
With laughter and giggles, we all confess.
In swirls and patterns, we celebrate fun,
In this joyful dance, we're all number one!

The Symphony of Metal and Stone

In a drawer full of jingle, oh what a sound,
Metallic laughter loops as they dance around.
Rings of gold and silver play hide-and-seek,
Clinking and clanking, what a quirky peek!

A floral bangle claims it's the queen of the pile,
While a chunky cuff grins, 'I'm just here for style!'
Together they chatter with gossip galore,
Creating a symphony that we can't ignore!

Fragments of a Festive Heart

A sparkle here, a shimmer there, oh what a sight,
A party of colors that twinkle so bright.
Charming chaos in a playful display,
Each piece tells a story, oh what can I say!

Earrings with flair waltz under the light,
While a single bracelet decides to take flight.
They giggle and jive, so merry and free,
Crafting an anthem for fun-loving spree!

Woven in Whispering Hues

Stripes of color tangled, they squabble, they tease,
'I'm the star of the show!' says the one made with beads.
But another chimes in, 'I shine with allure!'
In this vibrant skirmish, what piece is more pure?

Melodies wrap 'round the wrist and the neck,
Like a parade that's just waiting to deck.
Each stitch tells a tale, each hue holds a grin,
Lost in this charm, oh where do we begin?

The Rhythm of Hidden Stories

Underneath layers of fabric, they spin tales galore,
Each trinket a whisper, each charm opens a door.
The tales of grand feasts and dances at night,
Echo in laughter, shining warm with delight.

Oh, the secrets they hold, these treasures so bright,
A playful saga told in the soft, twinkling light.
With each gentle jingle, a dance comes alive,
In this funky ensemble, oh how we thrive!

Echoes of the Elegance

In a drawer, they jingle loud,
Colorful circles, good for a crowd.
My cat thinks they're toys galore,
Chasing the sound, always wanting more.

But when I wear them, they slip and slide,
Every wave feels like a ride.
Dancing at parties, looking so fine,
Crashing into friends, it's all part of the line.

When I'm cooking, what a scene!
They clang and clash, oh what a dream!
Spattering sauce with every swing,
My kitchen's a symphony, hear the bling!

So here's to the joy they bring to me,
A clumsy ballet, oh can't you see?
Life's a dance, a funny spree,
With colorful chaos, wild and free.

Adrift in Glass and Gold

Little loops of shimmer, oh what a sight,
On my wrist, they tinkle right.
Every gesture, a symphony played,
But watch out, for they might cascade!

While trying to sip my tea with grace,
They leap and jingle, oh what a race!
A little hiccup, a daring dance,
Hot tea spills, oh what a chance!

Neighbors peek through the window's frame,
Wondering if I'm going insane.
Practicing my moves, like a star on stage,
Yet tripping over pride, what a funny age!

So here's to these jewels of jolly mischief,
Turning calm days into comic relief.
Life's a circus with a bracelet show,
Sparkling laughter wherever I go.

The Dance of Shimmering Dreams

Each twirl sends them flying high,
A clattering song, oh me, oh my!
They wish to be free, I can tell,
Leaping off fingers, casting a spell.

Stepping outside with a daring flair,
Dancing through puddles without a care.
They whisper secrets of joyous pride,
As I stumble down the bumpy ride.

In the market, a charming sight,
Jesters of glass in the sunlight.
They sparkle and giggle, a wild parade,
While I juggle veggies, my mask unmade!

So let them ring, let them chime,
In this goofy dance, oh what a rhyme.
A playful waltz for these sparkling things,
Painting my days with the joy they bring.

Resonance of Radiant Rings

Wrapped in colors, a joyful stack,
On my fingers, they never lack.
There's a knock at the door, I run to greet,
Clanging like a wind chime, oh what a feat!

My friends make jokes, they can't contain,
"Are you leading a band or simply insane?"
With every step, an orchestra plays,
As I glide through life in melodious ways.

While grocery shopping, they love to shout,
"Look at her dance, what's this about?"
They chime and jive, a chorus alive,
Turning chores to shows, oh how they thrive!

So raise a toast to this musical art,
For life's more amusing with rhythm and heart.
A glorious ruckus, a vibrant sing,
In the joy of motion, hear the bling!

Brilliantly Bound

In a shop of colors, bright and bold,
Strawberry reds and marigold,
I picked a set that jingled loud,
Surrounded by the curious crowd.

My wrist looked like a music band,
Playing tunes at my command,
But when I waved, oh what a sight,
They flew off like birds in flight!

Friends laughed and begged for just one piece,
"Please wear them, let our joy increase!"
I tossed a few like candy treats,
Now all my pals are on their feets!

So we danced like stars in a night sky,
With clanging chimes, oh me, oh my!
Who knew my arms could make such sound,
Just when I thought my grace was found!

Circular Tales of Time

Round and round they twist and spin,
A history of laughter trapped within,
From the closet to my wrist they march,
Like a circus troupe under the arch.

A friend once claimed they're made of glue,
To keep my wrist from flowing through,
But when I slipped and fell intent,
They bounced away with great intent!

Chasing them felt like a wild race,
Rolling down the hallway, oh what a chase!
They laughed at me—a clever crew,
And hid beneath that old shoe too!

Now I wear them with a silly grin,
They jingle loud where I've been,
Every roll a tale to share,
Of laughter, chaos, and some flair!

Stars Encased in Jewels

In a box of sparkles, my treasures gleam,
Each one a wish, a childhood dream,
Shiny orbs that dance and sway,
I wear them proudly, come what may.

A clink and a clatter, what a sound!
Echoes of joy all around,
One slipped off during my tea,
Now it rolls away, just like me!

Among the crumbs and bits of cake,
I dive to catch that shiny snake,
Laughter spilling like the brew,
While my friends shout, "Who knew?"

So here's to jewels that sparkle bright,
And tales of antics, pure delight,
With each adornment, a little laughter,
Making moments that we chase after!

Adorned Journeys

My journey starts with a jingle bell,
On every road, I've tales to tell,
Adorned like a Christmas tree,
With every step, I giggle with glee!

A scrappy pair from a dusty stall,
Fun designs that make me stand tall,
A compliment here, a wink from there,
In vibrant hues, I shed my care!

Each step's a dance, a skipping game,
My jewels keep calling—fun's their name,
They flash like neon in the sun,
Creating moments that weigh a ton!

So here I prance, with jangly cheer,
Joy coated like candy, oh so near,
For with each journey, life's a ball,
And laughter's the best adornment of all!

Rich Tapestries of Touch

In a shop filled with shiny bling,
A catwalk model did her thing.
She slipped on a bracelet like a pro,
And tripped on the sequins, what a show!

A jester laughed with a twinkle in eye,
Who knew that jewels could cause a sigh?
Spinning around, he lost a shoe,
And said, "At least my sparkle still stays true!"

Up and down, they danced a spree,
With bangles rattling, feeling so free.
Twirling each other in a wacky waltz,
In the chaos, who's counting faults?

Gold and silver, a colorful mess,
Decorating laughter, truly the best.
In a twist of fate, they're tangled on floor,
But who needs grace when you've got more?

The Infinite Loop of Love

Two hearts met in a quirky shop,
Lost in treasures, they couldn't stop.
She wore a dozen rings on her hands,
He joked, "Do you need more to make your plans?"

Each spin gave her an unexpected jolt,
His giggles turned to an uproarious bolt.
Caught in a whirl of shimmering might,
They laughed as the jewels danced in the light.

He tried to impress with a grand display,
But tangled himself in a playful way.
"Is this a date or a circus show?"
She winked and said, "Just let it flow!"

Around and around, in a dizzy gaze,
They forgot the world, lost in a craze.
With laughter echoing, they'd always find,
Their playful hearts, perfectly aligned.

Ethereal Accents of Joy

In a whimsical world of glitter and glow,
A lady danced, putting on quite a show.
Her bracelet jingled, a comical sound,
As she tripped over her own frilly gown.

Tickled by laughter, the crowd cheered her on,
"Is that your outfit or the unicorn's spawn?"
A wink and a twirl, she responded in style,
While juggling gems and making them smile.

In a game of tag with her sparkling dress,
She chased her best friend through vibrant excess.
With each twist and turn, more laughter arose,
"Who knew such chaos could come from a pose?"

Amidst the giggles and hues so bright,
They spun and danced into the night.
Creating joy with every jangle and jump,
In a joyous loop, never a grump!

Synchronicity in Silver

In a shop filled with glitter, oh so bright,
I found a pair that just felt right.
They jingled and jangled, a merry tune,
While making me dance like a lunatic raccoon.

Friends laughed as I wobbled, all out of sync,
With silver companions, they seemed to wink.
'You're a festive chime!' they cried with glee,
As my arms twirled around, wild and free.

Each twist of my wrist, a clanging sound,
Beads bounced like popcorn, flying all around.
"Are you a fashionista or circus act?"
With every misstep, my confidence cracked.

But joy was the message, in metallic clinks,
Who cares if my style was missing links?
A silver laughter echoed, loud and clear,
In a world where fashion should bring good cheer.

Luminescent Layers

Layers stacked high, a dazzling sight,
A rainbow explosion, oh so light.
With colors that pop, like confetti in flight,
I felt like a cupcake, sprinkles and bright.

"Oh dear!" said my friend, "you look quite a treat!"
"Just a fashion statement, not candy to eat!"
But who could resist a munch or a nibble,
When bracelets glow like a disco ball dribble?

Each arm a canvas, a playful art,
Twirling and swirling, a dance from the heart.
They clatter together, a chorus of cheer,
I'm a walking parade, with laughter so near.

The neighbors peep out, with curious glee,
"Is that a new trend?" they ponder and see.
While I shimmy and shake, with humor abound,
In layers of laughter, joy knows no bound.

Embrace of Ancient Craft

In a market bustling with vibrant sights,
I chanced upon treasures of ancient delights.
Crafted with care from a time long past,
They whispered of stories, each piece built to last.

I tried on engagement, of woven gold fate,
But they clashed with my style—a disastrous date!
The artisan laughed, "It's your spirit that shines,"
As I twirled like a peacock, drawing all lines.

With each piece I donned, I felt so grand,
Yet looked like a tower that wobbled on sand.
"Fashion faux pas!" my friends all did shout,
As I strutted like royalty, filled with doubt.

But hey, who needs rules in a world full of fun?
Each tangled chain jingle simply adds to the run.
In a dance of tradition and laughter so free,
I embraced the mishaps, just being me.

Golden Echoes of Heritage

In a box of wonders, gleaming so bright,
Lay treasures untouched, oh what a sight!
Gold whispers of ancestors, all lined in a row,
Yet I tripped on a clasp, and put on a show.

"Look at you, a royal mess!" they quipped with a grin,
As I laughed in response, "Let the circus begin!"
Each golden ring wrapped like a bracelet of fun,
Perfectly paired with my quirky run!

I glittered and sparkled, a sight to behold,
Yet danced like a penguin in sandals of gold.
"Are you hosting a gala, or lost at the fair?"
A parade of chuckles flowed through the air.

But in every blunder, the laughter took flight,
Heritage mingled with joy—what a night!
With echoes of gold, I swaggered along,
Singing my heart out—a most comical song.

www.ingramcontent.com/pod-product-compliance
Lightning Source LLC
Chambersburg PA
CBHW062110280426
43661CB00086B/437